peace is...

women imagine a peaceful world

Jennifer deGroot

To the converted
Love,
Cate
2003

Peace is...women imagine a peaceful world

Published by Mennonite Central Committee Canada
134 Plaza Drive
Winnipeg, Manitoba
R3T 5K9
Website: www.mcc.org

With support from Canadian International Development Agency, NGO Division

Designed by Roberta Fast of Sandalwood Design
Printed by Harris Printing

ISBN 0-9688385-1-0

Proceeds from the sale of this book will be used to ensure that each person who has contributed in words or image will receive a copy of her own. Remaining proceeds will be directed to Mennonite Central Committee programs that contribute to women and peace in Asia and Africa.

The following words and images were
gathered in India, Chad, Niger, Senégal,
South Africa, Lesotho, and Uganda
between January and July 2000.

You are invited to engage with the people you will meet, to walk with them for a few moments listening to the messages of skin and voice, messages of determination, frustration, fatigue, delight, and an insistence that the world be a better place for the next generation.

"Women know what they want and think.
They are not doormats…
A woman may keep quiet
but she will burst and talk one day.
When she does people will say,
'She's right, she has tolerated it
for a long time.'"

Eunice Oyet
Uganda

peace is...

a world in which women can
speak boldly with heads held high

"Not by charity,
nor by sympathy,
but through our hard work
and our integrity,
we shall strive for our dignity."

Women at Ankur Kala
India

peace is...

a world in which women can
work together openly for their
rightful place in society

"I am a girl
but I am educated.
I go out and learn things
even if I am a girl."

Unmarried woman
India

peace is...

a world in which women and
girls have full opportunities
for learning

"When a child suffers —
if he is sick and you don't
have enough money —
that is a woman's problem.
And when the child is hungry
and the child goes to sleep crying
and hungry…that happened to me a lot."

Emily Thakane Nthonyana
Lesotho

peace is...

a world in which women can choose how many children to have and are able to provide fully for them

"Who has more sorrow in life?"
"Women.
Because they have so much work
and they are confined to the home."
"Who has more joy in life?"
"Women.
Because they have the joy
of having children and of
being with the family."

Women of Tamluk village
India

peace is...

a world in which women
and men share the joy
and responsibility of
raising children

"When you are economically self-sufficient you gain respect."

Mary Kaddu and Angela Ajeso
Uganda

peace is...

a world in which women have
their own source of income

"The happiest day of my life was
when I entered this house.
I didn't expect it at all."

Margaret Nakayiba
Uganda

peace is...

a world in which women are free
to own homes and property

"Now we are at the point
where women are owning property,
whereas before,
women were part of the property."

Workshop participants
Uganda

peace is...

a world in which women are not
treated as commodities

Female representation
in national parliament:

Uganda	33%
South Africa	30%
Canada	21%
India	9%
Niger	1%

peace is...

a world in which women are
fully represented in all levels
of leadership

Across the world,
the most dangerous place
for a woman to be
is in her own home.

peace is...

a world in which women are safe
within their own homes and free
to come and go at will

"The men listen to us but then
they deceive and cheat us
because they are the authority.
Eventually we just sit and watch.
We fear being beaten."

Women of Awer Camp
Uganda

peace is...

a world in which girls grow up
knowing their bodies will always
be sacred and safe

"In my tribe the men went to my Member of Parliament and asked how the government could take away their right to beat their wives. That was only two weeks ago."

Workshop participant
Uganda

30

peace is...

a world in which women are
fully recognized and protected
by the law

At one clinic in India,
7997 out of 8000
aborted fetuses were female.

peace is...

a world in which female life
is valued and celebrated

"When I became aware of the value of women, I first had to implement changes in my own family. First of all, I had to learn to treat my sons and daughters the same way."

Puspa Xalxo
India

peace is...

a world in which girls are
allowed to be children too

"I try to be an example
and raise my children differently
but one time my daughters-in-law saw
me with a jerry can on my head.
They were shocked and said my wife
must be very ill and they refused to
let me carry water."

Benjamin Oballim
Uganda

peace is...

a world in which women and
men share in the benefits and
burdens of work

"No, things will never change.
Women will always have to
give in to the man.
They will always be suppressed.
Women will always bear this sorrow."

Young married woman
India

peace is...

a world in which women are free
to have their own ideas and
determine their own future

"God has given us feet to walk,
hands to work,
mouths to speak.
Why aren't you using these?
Why should I go talk on your behalf?
How long do you want to keep
your mouths shut like a
bunch of newly-married brides?"

President of Women's Trust Fund
India

peace is...

a world in which women are
valued for their own strength
and intelligence rather than
their marital status

"When you're lucky enough
to have a man who understands you,
you have to protect him!"

Rachel Bassemda
Chad

peace is...

a world in which women and
men relate freely and equally

"What do I think about while I work?
Nothing, there's only work.
Thinking won't make things any easier.
Why think?"

Old woman
India

peace is...

a world in which women are
inspired to hope and imagine

"When I became a widow
I did not go back to the village.
I already had six children.
How could I go and start over with
another man who might also die?
I have been a widow for nine years.
Men say to me,
'What, no one has come to take over?'
I say, 'Take over what?'"

Diana
Uganda

peace is...

a world in which widows
and childless women can live
with dignity

"Now we're starting to see that we
can go out with our husbands,
even eat with them. The old women
give us a hard time for this but we ask
them, 'Were you happy then?…
Well then let us do things differently.'"

Rachel Bassemda
Chad

peace is...

a world in which women
of all ages learn from each
other's experiences

"Our culture has always been used as a scapegoat to justify discrimination against women. I try to challenge people and suggest that lots of things have changed since the days we were wearing animal skins. But they don't want to listen."

Sizane Ngubane
South Africa

peace is...

a world in which culture
liberates instead
of binds

"Even though there are pressures,
you must be joyful.
You must laugh."

Old woman
India

peace is...

a world in which women have
time for leisure and laughter

peace is...

a world in which all women
have both names and faces

author's words

Six months, seven countries, hundreds of women, countless images... This book is a surprise ending to a journey that took me to India, Chad, Niger, Senégal, South Africa, Lesotho, and Uganda between January and July 2000. The purpose of my travels was a gender analysis project for Mennonite Central Committee, an international relief and development agency. As I travelled I had no idea that a compilation such as this would result. I simply moved from place to place asking questions, listening to conversations, watching closely, creating photographs, and trying to understand the mysteries of life portrayed in skin and word.

When I returned to Canada I knew there was a story that needed to be told, a story beyond the faceless and nameless reports and recommendations. For six months I had walked on sacred ground and for myself and in respect of the women, children and men who so graciously shared their stories with me, I needed to say more.

Peace is often described simply as the absence of war. Peace is what men come and put together after things have been broken. By this interpretation, work that women do before, during, and after a war is not part of peace or peace building. It's simply what women do. Near the end of my journey I spent some time with women in northern Uganda who were living through a war that was nearly two decades old and showed little sign of ending. These women challenged me to see their work as creators and sustainers of life during times of war and peace, as peace building.

I listened to the words of the Ugandan women and thought back to all the other women I had met. All along the way, women had told me what their kind of peaceful world would look like. It would not just be a world without war. It would also be a world of physical and sexual safety, a world of political, economic, and social equality, a world in which they were free to represent themselves in government, to go to school, to have time to sit back and rest and hope in tomorrow. This is the story I share.

The people in these photos knew they were being photographed and quoted, and nodded their permission. However, they did not know that their words and images would become a book. Names, locations, and stories are what I recall from notes, photographs, and memory and any errors and omissions are entirely my responsibility. I hope that by some measure of grace, I am representing the people in this book fairly, and in a way that brings justice and honour.

Jennifer deGroot
Winnipeg, 2001.

notes

P. 20 ~ *The happiest day of my life…*
(see 21)

P. 22 ~ *Now we are at the point…*
This comment comes out of a conversation I had
with a group of women at St Jude Rural Training
Centre for Sustainable Integrated Organic
Agriculture near Masaka, who were studying
poultry for a week. After our discussion, the
women rose to sing the Uganda Women's
Anthem:

    Mothers, daughters
    All women everywhere
    Stand up and embrace your roles today

    We are the proud mothers of the nation
    The backbone without which it cannot stand
    We wake up at the crack of dawn
    And feed our nation with our brains
    With love and joy we care for our baby
    Uganda

P. 24 ~ *Female representation in national
parliament.*
These numbers represent elected rather than
appointed representatives and therefore do not
include the Canadian Senate. South Africa and
Uganda have achieved higher percentages
because they have implemented special measures
to ensure greater participation of women and
other marginalized groups such as people living
with disabilities. For example, Uganda has 56
seats specifically allotted to women.
For statistics from other countries, see
http://www.ipu.org/wmne/classif.htm.

P. 26 ~ *Across the world…*
In India, every 102 minutes a woman is killed in a
dowry death (see p.32). Fifty percent of Ugandan
women are regularly abused by their husbands. In
Canada, fifty percent of women and girls
experience some form of physical or sexual
violence. Of these assaults, half occur in the
home. *(Based on statistics from numerous sources)*

P. 28 ~ *The men listen to us…*
Most of the women at Awer Camp for Displaced
people near Gulu town in northern Uganda have
been in the camp for nearly five years. The
women do all the work in the camp as well as
work in the fields, while the men play cards and
drink. "When you're redundant you resort to
things like that", the women explained. Their
sense of humour was contagious.

P. 17 ~ Men and women sat
separately to listen to the
presentation by the Social Unit
for Community Health and
Improvement (SUCHI)
working in Chittoor District,
the province of Andhra
Pradesh, India. Bala Sundaram,
one of SUCHI's community
workers said to me, "A community is made of both men and
women… It can't say it is
developed if only the men have
been affected."

P. 21 ~ Margaret Nakayiba was
my neighbour in the Kampala
neighbourhood where I stayed in
Uganda. She is a single parent to
six children. I had two long
conversations with her and at
the end of the first I asked her,
"Margaret, what was the best day
of your life?" I said I'd come back
for the answer and I also invited
her to give me a question to
ponder during that time. She
asked, "Would you ever marry a
black man?" A month or so later
I went back and she gave me this
answer. In response to her
question I said, "I don't know,
it's hard to marry someone who's
not from your own culture."
Margaret said, "That's not a
good enough reason."

P. 19 ~ This woman in Andhra
Pradesh province, India has
received a pregnant cow as part
of a government program
encouraging women's self-
sufficiency.

P. 23 ~ In Africa women are
frequently judged by the number
of cows they are deemed to be
worth. This is Mama Diza, the
mother of Diza (see p 13). She
is standing with her cow. I
asked Diza's husband why he
picked this woman to be his wife
and he said shyly, "I knew that
she could work hard." From my
vantage point, they both worked
hard caring for their four
children, their animals, and the
land which provided possibly
the most wonderful food I've
ever eaten, including pineapples
and papayas picked minutes
before they were served.

P. 30 ~ In my tribe...

Another of the workshop participants I met at St. Jude's (see page 22) made this comment to me. My Ugandan friend Grace told me of a man she'd met who was complaining about women these days. "You can't even hit them, even your own wife," he said. The organization that is leading the struggle against domestic violence is FIDA, a worldwide federation of women lawyers.

P. 32 ~ At one clinic...

This statistic was found in a Calcutta newspaper during my time in India. Dowry, or the payment a bride's family must make to her in-laws, was repeatedly explained to me as the root cause of much of women's oppression in India. This custom is in stark contrast to the bride price that men's families pay to women's families in Africa as compensation for the worth or value of a woman that needs to be replaced if she leaves the family. Dowry demands are exacerbated by commercialism; dowry is often measured today in expensive imported cars and VCRs instead of locally produced jewellery and sarees. Unfortunately dowry does not end at the wedding. Many bridegrooms and their families continue to demand more and more dowry years after the marriage. When these dowry demands are not met, dowry deaths are common. These deaths are usually covered up as gas stove "accidents" and are perpetrated by the husband or the in-laws or are the result of the wife's desperate suicide. Because of the dowry custom, many families have difficulty celebrating the birth of a daughter. A newspaper clipping from January 2000 reports:

> Last week a tragedy uniquely Indian in dimension struck the small town of Bhilai. Four daughters of a poor family committed suicide to relieve their parents of the "burden" of marrying them off. They left behind a simple note, saying they could not bear to see their family crumble under the burden of trying to find husbands for them.

P. 34. When I became aware...

Puspa Xalxo has four children, two daughters and two sons. She was hired as the first female field worker for Jan Utthan Samiti (People's Development Committee) after MCC India suggested that the organization show more gender sensitivity. Puspa told me, "At the beginning I was pushed into leadership. I was very nervous. I would cry. It was not an easy struggle. But now I want them to push me." Hari, one of the project coordinators, explained, "We weren't pushing from the back, but from the head and the heart."

P. 25 ~ Anne-Claude Rossier is a pastor in the Reformed Church in Switzerland. Lihle Dlamini heads the Domestic Violence desk at the Pietermaritzburg Agency for Christian Social Awareness (PACSA) in Pietermaritzburg, South Africa.

P. 29 ~ Two girls in Midnapore, West Bengal, India (see also p. 32).

P. 33 ~ These small girls are 'learning the taste of school' at their pre-primary school near McCluskie Gunj, Bihar province, India. Inside the school they sing a coal workers' folk song:

> Flowers are beautiful
> Our youth is passing
> It's not beautiful like the flowers
> It's full of struggle.

P. 27 ~ Three unmarried women in Midnapore, West Bengal, India. The question I was most asked by women in India was, "Who let you come here?"

P. 31 ~ This Basotho woman entrepreneur sold me some fruit along the side of the road near Roma. In Lesotho, women are still considered minors under the law, meaning a woman's 18-year-old son can own property and vote while she cannot. At the time of my visit, a Married Person's Equality Bill was being negotiated.

P. 35 ~ In Asia and Africa, girls as young as three years old learn the role of mother.

P.36 ~ I try to be an example...
Oballim has been repeatedly elected as leader of the Awer Camp for Displaced People. When I arrived, he took time to show me the camp, mentioning quietly to all of the women we passed that I wanted to talk with them when we were through and to meet under the big tree in a short while. When we returned to the tree I was shocked to see 250 women eagerly awaiting me. Benjamin opened the visit with prayer and sat quietly beside me during our discussion, interrupting only to suggest that perhaps if the women didn't all shout at the same time I might be able to hear them better.

P. 38 ~ No, things will never change...
(see page 39)

P. 40~ God has given...
This woman (pictured on p.41) is president of the Panchratna Mahila Vikas Trust (Five Jewels Women's Development Trust) (see also page 15). The red line in her hair signifies that she is married. At the meeting I attended, the women discussed government programs that were available to them but were not being implemented by the regional government official. When they suggested that the president be the one to approach the man and demand justice, she responded with these words.

P. 42 ~ When you're lucky enough...
Rachel Bassemda was active in forming an association of Christian women in Chad through which she educates both men and women on issues of women's equality. A dignified and joyful woman, Madame Rachel attributes the success and happiness of her marriage to the fact that she had a fiancé before she had a husband and so they were able to discuss things together beforehand.

P. 44 ~ What do I think about...
The old woman in Tamluk village who said this to me is a single mother of seven daughters and one son. She also told me: "If my husband had stayed with me, maybe I wouldn't have had to slog so hard."

P. 46 ~ When I became a widow...
Diana is the director of the Gulu Vocational and Community Institute where she tries hard to educate both women and men to be healthy contributors to society.

P. 37 ~ These semi-nomadic Fulani women in Niger are returning from their afternoon trip to the well.

P. 41 ~ See P. 40

P. 45 ~ This proud Ugandan mother, a farmer near Masaka, told me that her burden is increased because her husband is disabled.

P. 47 ~ I forget the details of this woman whom I met in a semi-nomadic camp in Niger. I remembered only that she killed a chicken for our supper and dressed in purple to be photographed.

P. 39 ~ I met this woman in Tamluk village, West Bengal. When I asked her if she thought the situation of women would ever change, she responded with these words. Her air was defiant and proud and she held onto this truth as if her femaleness and all that it entailed was the only thing that truly belonged to her.

P. 43 ~ Glory and Paul Vijaya-kumar are educators, medical professionals, and community activists who formed the Social Unit for Community Health and Improvement (SUCHI) which has been active in Chittoor District, Andhra Pradesh, India since 1980. Their work includes education, mobilization, vocational training, literacy, conflict resolution, environmental, agricultural and alternative energy training, and the promotion of women's equality throughout all of these activities.

The border design and symbol comes from the Ashanti people in Ghana and signifies "strength".

Jennifer deGroot (pictured here with Mary Magdalen, Sarai, and Jeba Mani in Chittoor District, Andhra Pradesh, India) lives in Winnipeg and imagines a world in which we all have the opportunity to walk a few moments in each other's sarees.

P. 49 ~ Shuvra Chatarjee and Joyce Victor are both teachers at Ankur Kala, a girls training centre in Calcutta, India (see p.10)

P. 51 ~ Woman at the well in Tamluk village, West Bengal, India.

P. 53 ~ I met this woman in a camp for disabled people 20 or so kilometres outside of Niamey, Niger. The camp is divided into four sections according to different disabilities: physical, visual, auditory, and those suffering from leprosy. Family members of the disabled persons also live in the camp. The sense of community was very strong and the laughter flowed freely.

P. 54 ~ This woman is a household helper in Senégal. She was probably recruited from a rural area to work in the home of a wealthier family in the city. The millions of women and girls who do this work in Africa receive extremely low wages and are at great risk of exploitation and abuse.